NONVIOLENCE

Explained to My Children

NONVIOLENCE

Explained to My Children

Jacques Sémelin

TRANSLATED BY
Leah Brumer

MARLOWE & COMPANY
NEW YORK

NONVIOLENCE EXPLAINED TO MY CHILDREN

Copyright © Éditions du Seuil 2000
Translation Copyright © Leah Brumer 2002

Published by
Marlowe & Company
An Imprint of Avalon Publishing Group Incorporated
161 William Street, 16th Floor
New York, NY 10038

First published as *La nonviolence expliquée à mes filles* by
Éditions du Seuil in France in 2000. This edition
published by arrangement with Éditions du Seuil.

Library of Congress Cataloging-in-Publication Data
is available.

9 8 7 6 5 4 3 2 1

Paperback ISBN 1-56924-515-0
Hardcover ISBN 1-56924-514-2

Designed by Pauline Neuwirth, Neuwirth & Associates, Inc.

Printed in Canada
Distributed by Publishers Group West

Contents

PREFACE

"**D**ad, nonviolence is a strange word. Can you explain it?"

I've spent nearly twenty years studying violence and nonviolent action. How am I going to answer that question from my 14- and 8½-year-old daughters?

We sat down together with a book about Martin Luther King, Jr. and African-Americans' struggles for civil rights. I listened to their reactions and wrote down their questions. Most had to do with daily life. If someone tries to beat me up, what do I do? What about kids at school who try to steal from me? What about sexual abuse? Youth violence? Racism? To answer, I set my precious studies aside. That's how I started writing. I gave the first few pages to my daughters to read and then began revising.

I wanted to tell them that nonviolence is not passivity. It's a way of being and behaving which seeks to resolve conflicts, fight injustice, and build lasting peace. To illustrate those ideas, I drew on examples from everyday life and from history.

JACQUES SÉMELIN

NONVIOLENCE

Explained to My Children

NONVIOLENCE

Explained to My Children

Nonviolence is a strange word. Can you explain it?

It's easier to explain violence than nonviolence. You know right away what violence is when you see it happen: people hit each other, bombs explode, blood flows. But what is nonviolence? It's silent. It's invisible.

People think a nonviolent person is a pacifist, someone who rejects war. They believe nonviolent people are cowards who don't want to fight. Since violence is all around us, they think that if you're nonviolent, you have your head in the clouds and let people walk all over you. "I'm nonviolent. Go ahead, do whatever you want to me. Peace, brother!"

But that's not nonviolence.

So what is it?

It's a way of being and of behaving in conflict situations that respects the other person. That's a basic definition. I'd like to give you several examples to help explain what it means.

It's a way of dealing with conflict? It's not about being passive?

Not at all. It's true that the word itself—nonviolence—could lead you to think that. Obviously, it means saying "no" to violence. That's the first and most obvious element of nonviolence: don't hit or mistreat other people and, of course, don't rape or kill anyone. Everyone understands that. When the subject comes up in newspaper articles, it always means "no violence." Once I even saw a funny advertisement for a detergent described as nonviolent. It said, "Buy this soap because it won't beat up your clothes"! Today you hear people talk about nonviolent video games in which you don't have to kill your enemy to win.

But nonviolence includes a second element: action. If you're going to confront violence effectively, you've got to be active. In fact, you've got to be very active. That's not always clear when you use the term, so it makes more sense to talk about nonviolent action or active nonviolence.

Nonviolence means acting against violence without using violence. How do you do that? There are thousands of ways. Some are painful and difficult but others can be funny. Yes, there is humor in this approach. Nonviolence also uses what we might call "the force of life" to win. When you use violence, the threat of death—the other person's death—is always present.

But how do you fight without violence? That seems pretty hard to me!

When people really want to fight, they often end up using violence. Violence and war are deeply rooted in our history. Movies and comic books show that violence is the way to dominate other people and that it works. If you have more weapons, you can order people to obey you because you can scare them. Being the strongest often means being the most violent.

Even so, history shows us there were times when events didn't work out like that, when people didn't want to obey any longer even if they were scared and when the weakest and poorest tried to defend themselves without weapons. Does that sound unbelievable? But what else could they do? Let's say you have nothing—no guns, no tanks. If you try to obtain weapons, you know your adversary will always be better armed. So you've got to defend yourself differently. You have to learn to be strong without being violent. You could call it "the power of the weak." It's mysterious, but I've studied it to try to understand it.

O.K., give me an example.

One of the most famous examples is Martin Luther King, Jr.'s, struggle for civil rights for black people. There's a good illustrated book about him. We can talk about it if you like.

It all started in 1955. There was tremendous racism and racial segregation in the southern United States. Blacks were not allowed to mix with whites. For example, when black people rode the bus they had to sit in the back and leave the seats in front for whites. Black people didn't have the right to go into certain restaurants or cafés. Sometimes there were signs that said "No coloreds or dogs." White extremists would attack, beat and even kill black people.

But one day an extraordinary event took place in Montgomery, Alabama, a very racist town. It began with something simple. On December 1, 1955, a black seamstress, Rosa Parks, was on her way home from work. She was very tired. When she boarded the bus, instead of sitting in back like she was supposed to, she sat in front. A white person who wanted to sit in her seat complained to the bus driver. "What's that dirty colored woman doing in the white people's seats?" The police arrested her. A black passenger hurried to pay her fine so she wouldn't have to go to jail. But Rosa Parks was still angry. You'd say, "She was really fed up." She wouldn't go along with segregation any more. Together with the passenger who'd helped her, she decided to go see Martin Luther King, Jr., a young black pastor who'd just come to Montgomery. He was twenty-six, married, and the father of his first child.

King wasn't willing to accept segregation any longer either. He wanted things to change, too. Of course, black people weren't slaves like they had been a century earlier. They were free. But in reality, every day white people humiliated them and treated them like dogs. King had the energy to take on the fight but he didn't want to use violence. So what would he do?

The next evening, King and some of his friends held a meeting. They agreed it was time for change. All of a sudden, someone had a great idea: "Let's organize a boycott and all refuse to take the bus! When the [white-owned] bus company sees they're losing money, they'll treat us better." The next day, King and the others asked the city's black residents to stay off the buses. "Don't take the bus to work, to school or to go downtown." The boycott worked immediately. The buses ran empty, or nearly empty. But black people had to organize to make it effective. To get around the city, people would carpool or take taxis. Many walked, even if they had to go several miles.

White people couldn't believe what was happening. "Those blacks think they've found a new game," they said. "But their feet are going to start hurting and then they'll give up." The most racist went on the attack. King regularly received threatening phone calls. Callers would say, "Dirty nigger trash, we're going to get you!" Then on January 30, 1956, a bomb exploded in front of his house. Luckily, no one was hurt. Black people wanted to take revenge and go after whites with weapons. But King stopped them. "I want you to go home and put down your weapons," he said. "We cannot solve this problem through retaliatory violence—We must love our white brothers, no matter what they do to us—We must meet hate with love." But it was hard. The police arrested King many times, jailed him, and then let him go. The racists wanted to find a way to destroy him but they couldn't accuse him of anything because he rejected violence.

The boycott lasted for months. The bus company didn't give in but the movement began to be known across the United States and abroad. Ordinary black people in Montgomery, not just King, became famous—and not for having done something violent. Finally, journalists were showing interest in them and black people were getting a chance to speak. They said, "We want the same rights as white people." On November 10, 1956, the U.S. Supreme Court ruled that bus segregation was unconstitutional because all citizens are equal. Black people won the right to sit next to whites. The boycott had lasted for three hundred and eighty-two days.

I like the woman in the book you showed me who said, "Before, my feet were rested but my soul was tired. Now my feet are tired but my soul is rested!" She walked miles every day but it didn't matter. She had her dignity.

I also like the part where black people won and King said to them, "I would be terribly disappointed if any of you go back to the buses bragging, 'We, the Negroes, won a victory over the white people.' We must take this not as victory over the white man but as a victory for justice and democracy—We are just going to sit where there's a seat."

Why do you like that?

Because it shows that they didn't want power, they wanted to be respected.

That's right. The goal of a nonviolent struggle is to win respect from other people. It's not just about winning rights, like being able to sit wherever you want on a bus. King also said, "We must act in such a way as to make possible a coming together of white people and colored people on the basis of a real harmony of interests and understanding. We seek an integration based on mutual respect." That's logical, isn't it? In 1997, a movement of French high school students came up with this slogan: "Respect is more powerful than violence."

Do you remember the basic definition of nonviolence I gave you? It says that nonviolence is a way of being. That way of being, or state of mind, refers to respect. It's not easy to respect other people. Respect begins within the family between parents and children and between brothers and sisters. Even adults don't always manage very well. We call each other all sorts of names and try to climb over other people, especially at work. You learn to stab people in the back so you can be the strongest, get to the top, and earn more money. We don't set a very good example for the young.

Even so, there are people who fight but still respect their adversaries. They believe in human beings or in God and they refuse to do certain things in the name of their principles or their faith. It's unusual, but it does happen. When we talk about them, we say you can trust their word. That means you can believe what they say. They don't think people should be treated like objects you can buy or sell. But these people are not naïve. They know how to defend themselves and succeed in life but they represent the spirit of nonviolence even if they've never heard the word.

So the basic message of nonviolence is, "Defend yourself but respect your adversary"?

Exactly.

You said that the nonviolent person rejects violence. But just what is violence?

To talk about nonviolence, you've got to start by recognizing the violence that's inside you. Everyone—boys and girls—can become violent, even very violent. Boys may fight more often but girls can be violent, too. For example, you can hurt someone with words. You can wound and humiliate them in public. You'd say, "Put them down" or "Disrespect them." Look how children sometimes amuse themselves by pulling the wings off insects, one by one, to see what it's like.

You know that human beings can attack people just like themselves and massacre them. The worst example is the German dictator, Adolf Hitler, the Nazis, and everyone who collaborated with them during World War II. Hitler ordered that millions of Jews, along with gypsies, disabled people, and homosexuals, be killed in gas chambers.

Do you think we can eliminate violence?

I'm not very optimistic about human nature.
After seeing Nazi concentration camps and the
ovens at Auschwitz, Poland, where human
beings were cremated, people said, "Never
again!" But it happened again in the 1990s in
Yugoslavia, Bosnia, and Kosovo. Thousands of
defenseless people—women, children, and old
people—were deported and killed. It's as if we
hadn't understood what was happening.

I don't think we'll ever manage to eliminate
violence but we can hold it back. And, luckily,
sometimes we do manage to live in peace. We
can control violence in the same way that a
cowboy reins in a bucking horse. But to do
that, you've really got to understand it.

It's a kind of energy that comes from inside us. There's nothing you can do about it.

Some people do think violence is a kind of
energy, an electric current that flows out of
the body that we're helpless to stop. According
to that way of thinking, violence is
everywhere and it's as natural as life. But don't
make the mistake of confusing strength and
violence. Even children can tell them apart.
When people say, "That man is strong!"

because he's got big muscles and can lift a piano by himself, they don't mean he's violent. Violence is a special form of strength that hurts, wounds, or kills, like a man who gets drunk and starts beating his wife.

By the same token, being ready to fight doesn't mean being violent. You need a fighting spirit to get ahead and establish yourself, whether in sports or at work. That doesn't mean you want to crush the other person, but that you want to succeed. A nonviolent fighting spirit certainly exists. Throughout his life, Martin Luther King, Jr., encouraged black people to develop that spirit. The day before he died, he made a speech in which he expressed his fighting spirit. "If something isn't done, and in a hurry, to bring the colored peoples of the world out of their long years of poverty, their long years of hurt and neglect, the whole world is doomed," he said. "We mean business now and we are determined to gain our rightful place in God's world."

If you get angry at someone, is that violence?

We'd probably call it aggressiveness, but some people do label it violence. I disagree. They would say if a young person or an adult speaks angrily, that qualifies as violence. No! That would mean that violence is whatever you can't tolerate any longer. But if you define the word too broadly, it ends up not meaning anything at all.

Everyone has experienced feelings of aggression. Sometimes getting mad and swearing can do you good. It's a way of saying you've had enough. That's it! No more! Who knows? It might even help you to start talking again with a grown-up or a friend.

So what do you really mean when you talk about violence?

Violence leads to denying another person's humanity and, ultimately, to his or her death. I'm not just talking about physical death, when the heart stops beating and the organs stop working, but about the death of the person's deepest self. You no longer see the other person as a human being but as an object or an animal that can be exploited, abused and killed.

Violence takes many forms, not just one. We usually think of physical violence as something caused by guns. We see that every day on TV or in the movies. But there are other forms of violence that aren't so easy to spot, like when people are humiliated, don't have a home, or a way to support themselves, or when no one says hello to them on the street anymore. That kind of violence can be very harmful even if it's silent. One day the person may react violently or commit suicide and everyone would seem so surprised. "What was wrong with her?" they ask. "Oh, well. We didn't have any idea." Combating violence isn't just about attacking the visible part of the iceberg. It's also about fighting misery and exclusion, injustice and inequality. Those are buried deeper.

I hope I'm not boring you with these definitions.

You still haven't told me what to do if someone comes after me.

You're right. Now it's my turn to ask you a question. If someone hit you at school, for example, what would you do?

I wouldn't just stand there. I'd say to the person, "Hey, you started it, but I'm going to finish it!"

That answer seems completely normal to me. All parents tell their children to defend themselves. But don't you think there's another way to respond besides striking back?

No, there isn't. Nonviolence doesn't let you defend yourself physically. Someone hits you and you're supposed to thank him!

No, not at all! Do you know what aikido is?

I've heard the word. I have a friend who does it.

It's a nonviolent martial art that ought to be better known. The principle is to defend yourself without attacking. You use your opponent's strength to throw her off balance so she can't fight. It's not just a powerful technique that lets you confront aggression, but also a state of mind based on respect for life. Aikido's goal is to "drain" the hostile intentions inside your opponent and without hurting her physically, to change her state of mind so that she no longer wants to cause harm.

Young people as well as children, women and the elderly can practice aikido. It teaches physical and psychological balance. Practicing aikido frees you from the fear of being abused or attacked because you know what to do if it does happen. You learn to look your attacker straight in the eye.

Of course if a boy in the schoolyard hits you, I wouldn't necessarily recommend that you get him in an aikido hold. But if other people know you have this skill, some of them will think twice before bothering you.

That's for sure!

Aikido is one option for responding to more serious situations but I have some other ideas, too. They're not all physical responses.

Like what?

To answer, I have to explain another important difference. I'm talking about the distinction between violence and conflict. A scuffle between buddies or an argument between parents isn't necessarily violence. It's normal not to always agree. But conflict and violence are not the same. Violence is a conflict that takes a wrong turn.

The problem is knowing how to behave in a conflict. What's the best way to act so that the other person still respects you, while keeping the situation from getting out of hand and turning violent? It's not easy. It's really too bad that we adults didn't learn how to do that when we were in school. The knowledge would've helped us throughout our whole lives. It would be great if the schools prepared you a little better.

Roughly speaking, there are three ways to behave if you're faced with a conflict. First, you can act as if nothing is wrong, remain passive, and behave as if everything will work out on its own. That's never a very smart gamble. Some day, the very same conflict could come back and hit you in the face.

Second, you could just blame the other person. You'd hold a grudge and respond aggressively or violently. We know from experience that violence seems to work—and fast. But the person who's lost the fight often wants to take revenge. So the conflict hasn't been resolved at all!

Third, you could find a solution acceptable to both. We call that a compromise. It assumes that each person will give in a little bit so that everyone wins something. That's the nonviolent approach to conflict. It's a good way to build long-term peace. Sometimes it can be pretty easy to reach an agreement—you just share what you had wanted to keep for yourself. But it can take time in complicated cases. You've got to stop hurting each other, try to explain your point of view, and really want to make peace. People don't always want to do that. Techniques like mediation can help. Here's some advice: whatever the conflict, try to use your imagination to come up with a solution that no one else has thought of. It helps to be creative—not just in advertising campaigns, but in solving conflicts, too.

But really, if someone hits me, I'm not going to turn the other cheek!

I would hope not. You're thinking of what Jesus said: "If anyone strikes you on the right cheek, turn the other also." That's difficult to interpret. It's hard enough not to retaliate if someone hits you. But if you offer the other cheek, that seems like a provocation. We can say for sure that Jesus was asking us not to act like our attacker. By behaving differently, we break one of the most powerful links in the chain of violence: imitation. We also have to find a way to relate what Jesus said to the very challenging Gospel passage that tells us to love our enemy. Martin Luther King, Jr., understood it this way: "There's something about love that builds up and is creative," he said. "There is something about hate that tears down and is destructive. So love your enemies."

Then what do you do?

Look how Jesus reacted after he was arrested and the officer slapped him. The official had criticized Jesus for the way he spoke to the high priest. Jesus' reaction was to question the man. "If I have spoken badly, show me how. If I have spoken well, why do you strike me?" Instead of offering the other cheek, he used words to appeal to his attacker's conscience.

You might think that responding with words instead of fists is a silly idea but it can be very effective. This is another aspect of nonviolence. We might all have a similar experience some day, whether or not we believe in God. Words set us free from violence. But I don't mean just any words. You can't shout or yell insults that show you're afraid. No, I mean honest words that can defuse tension. A little humor helps, too. Or a look. Without being aggressive, you can be very effective just by looking at someone straight in the eye.

For example?

I remember a true story that a psychologist friend told me. It's about a very tall girl who had a hard time because of her height. On the street, people would turn around as she went by and make fun of her. She ended up seeing this psychologist. Little by little, she gained self-confidence. One day, she passed two boys in the street. One said to the other, "Hey, I'd need a stepladder for a girl like that!" She turned toward him, looked directly at him and, without being mean, said, "Do you feel like you're that small?"

Of course, you need to have gained self-confidence to be brave enough to answer like that.

Yes, and that's not so easy. It's a lot simpler just to punch out the kid!

How do you gain self-confidence? Very few people have it when they're young. But you know, even when you get to be an adult, it's not necessarily any easier. I'm sorry, but I don't have a recipe for you. All I can do is tell you about my own experiences and point out a few paths you might take.

To gain self-confidence, you've got to discover the strength inside each of us. It's an internal strength built on each person's human dignity. If you've had painful experiences, you often have an easier time drawing on the resources from this strength. It's true from childhood. In general, when you've been humiliated or suffered what you feel is an injustice, you have two choices. First, you can feel resentful toward the rest of the world and try to seek revenge. If you take that route, you may become violent, or at least hostile. That's what we've been talking about. The other possibility is that little by little you learn to move beyond your suffering. As you progress, you feel yourself becoming stronger inside. Certain activities, like music, art, acting, or sports, can help you to express yourself. You might even develop a passion for math or French. Why not? Many young people find a way out like that. You don't necessarily forget what people have done to you but you manage to get control of your feelings.

You know, something very similar happened to me. By the time I started school, my eyesight was already pretty bad. There were some boys who called me "four eyes." One day, I don't know what came over me, but I told them I'd had it. I said that I was going to show them! I started working really hard at school. There are many stories like mine in which people try to transform their suffering into something positive as a way out of a difficult situation.

But you can't do that all by yourself.

At some point, another person will often help you to take control of yourself. Asking someone to listen to you is part of the nonviolent approach. But you've got to decide to reach out.

Daring to speak up and talk about your suffering and your fear takes real courage. Talking is a way to free yourself from your fears. It would be a mistake to keep them locked up because those feelings do the most harm if they stay inside. It's normal to feel fear. You've just got to learn to tame it. To free yourself from fear and ease your suffering, you've got to risk speaking out and speaking your own truth.

For example, if a girl or boy has been sexually abused, it's very important to be able to talk to a trusted friend, whether a young person or an adult. It's difficult but not shameful. Unfortunately, you do hear about young people being sexually abused by family members and other youths. Talking can be comforting. It helps you to gain some distance from what's happened and, in a way, start over. It's the same in the case of child abuse. Even if a child feels she is betraying her mother or father, she will be better off if she talks to someone.

But it's hard to do that.

True, it's hard not to feel like a victim. However, nonviolent solutions are possible only when the victim assumes responsibility for his own actions. The process begins when you refuse to be an easy mark for other people any longer.

When you decide you won't be a victim, you end a relationship in which you're the loser. You refuse to play the game that other people want you to play. When you stand up like that, you're saying, "That's it, I'm never going to take that again." You become the subject of your own life. You're in charge.

After all, children know what to do when a game turns violent. Someone yells, "Stop! You're hurting me! It's not funny anymore!" To stop people from hurting or harassing you, you've got to find the courage to say "no." A strong, firm "no" that shows you refuse to accept what they're doing to you.

But really, if someone's going to jump you, what do you suggest? There's a boy in my class who was just robbed again. The first time they took his jacket and the second time, his shoes. This time it was his knapsack.

And what do you think someone should do in that situation?

Well, give them what they want! You're not going to say, "Hey, that's a lousy thing to do. You must have had a hard time when you were little and your parents didn't pay enough attention to you." You're not going to play therapist!

Did this student talk to an adult right away about what happened to him?

From the beginning? I don't know.

When you've been robbed, you're a little ashamed. You've let someone else dominate you and you don't really want anyone else to find out. The kids who did it may be threatening you. "If you say anything, we're going to get you." So you keep quiet. If you do that, there's no reason it won't happen a second and a third time. Intimidation depends on the code of silence.

The only solution is to talk to an adult you trust right away, even if you've only been threatened. The only way to protect yourself is to break that code. Here again, taking a nonviolent approach means risking speaking up so you won't be a victim any more.

O.K., but the problem with this kid is that he looks like a victim. He's kind of wimpy. He wears thick glasses.

Are you saying it's his fault that he was robbed?

A little bit. It's not an accident that it happened to him.

It's true that kids who get attacked often fit the profile of a victim. Is it because of how they look? In part, yes. But it's mostly because they lack self-confidence. The bullies sense that they're easy targets. That's why it's so important to talk with these young people about what's happened to them so they don't put themselves in the position of being victims any longer.

But these attacks aren't a problem only for the child who's been robbed. They're also a problem for everyone else around who lets it happen. If the adults don't do anything, it's certainly their problem. But it's your problem, too, yours and the other students'. Who knows? One day it could happen to you. While this student is gaining self-confidence, you can follow a simple, and often very effective, strategy to keep him from being attacked again. When he leaves school, he should walk out with two or three friends. Being with other people can protect you.

Strength in numbers.

Exactly. Strength in numbers is an important principle of nonviolence. I'd like to tell you more about that. But first I promised to talk about mediation.

What is it exactly?

A way of helping to solve conflicts by making sure there are no winners and no losers. In short, everyone must be satisfied with the solution.

Mediation is useful for adults, for example, who are getting a divorce. But it can also be used with young people. Some middle schools are starting to use boys and girls as student mediators who intervene during recess.

How do they learn to do that?

They're trained. The first goal is to help them develop self-confidence and know themselves better. They also learn to listen. Knowing how to listen to others is a useful skill throughout life. They learn certain techniques during their training. For example, the "telephone game" teaches them how hard it is to really listen. In that game, someone says something to you,

you repeat it to the person next to you, who says it to the person next to her, and so on. When you come to the other end of the circle, the sentence has changed completely because no one really listened carefully.

The students also learn to understand and analyze what has taken place in a conflict. They do lots of practical exercises. They choose a conflict, act it out and examine different solutions. That gives them a better idea of how to intervene in the schoolyard.

They start by saying, "O.K., so can you tell me why you're fighting?" You try to listen closely to each person's point of view. But you've got to be careful. In mediation, you're not making judgments. You're not going to say, "You're wrong, you're a jerk, you shouldn't have done that." Instead, you try to understand what both people are feeling and help them find a solution. Mediating is like building a bridge between two banks of a river. Here it's a bridge between two people. The results are often surprising, even if the mediation isn't always successful. More serious conflicts can take time.

Mediators say that learning these techniques is very helpful. They use them in their daily lives—not only in school but with their families and friends, too.

But at school, the violence might be so serious that students can't resolve it on their own. Adults really need to intervene.

Absolutely. The level of violence is sometimes so high that everyone—teachers, students, and the entire school staff—must be mobilized. Some U.S. schools have put armed security guards in schools. Should we do that? I'm not sure that's the right answer. What's important is that adults intervene before it's too late. Otherwise, if teachers ignore signs of trouble, the situation can become dangerous. Young people with a tendency toward violence can become more violent over time. Here's an example someone gave me of an eighth-grader who attacked another student. None of the adults said anything to him. He went on to attack a teacher and still no one spoke up. Then he was absent from school for a long time. Even when he came back, no one said a word. Why not? Because some people thought he was unhappy at home and needed another chance. But giving him a real chance would have meant telling him that he'd crossed the line. He should have been punished in a way that would have helped him start over. Instead, no one did anything. His behavior got worse and he moved into crime and drugs. I really think this young man was asking adults to make him stop. He wanted them to say, "These are the rules. You must not cross this line." It's very important for adults to provide guideposts for young people.

So nonviolence goes hand in hand with the law?

Of course, and even with a certain kind of discipline. You don't look very happy about that. Obviously, it depends on the particular law. There are fair laws and unfair laws. When a law is unfair, like the one that required black people to sit in the back of the bus, it may be legitimate to disobey. That's called civil disobedience. Martin Luther King, Jr., organized that kind of action.

You can debate whether a particular law is good or bad. But that doesn't affect the main point: laws are necessary to prevent violence. To live together we need rules and landmarks, like a set of traffic rules that everyone must respect. When you drive a car, you need to know if you're supposed to drive on the right or left. I don't know whether it's better to drive on one side rather than the other, but I do know that horrible accidents would happen if everyone drove wherever they chose. Laws make it possible for us to keep a safe distance from each other as well as cross paths and respect other people.

But there are times when adults tell us to obey without explaining anything. They expect us to act like puppets.

That's an important point. Let's say a teacher stands in front of her students and says, "I am the authority. This is good, that is bad. You must obey me. No discussion!" There's a good chance no one will listen to her. That may have worked when I was in school and it was even more effective during your grandparents' time. But not anymore. Today we need a different kind of authority—one that is more respectful of everyone, that allows people to be heard, takes their views into account, and shows firmness when necessary. In other words, we need nonviolent authority.

Schools run better when students participate in making the rules. Often the first result is less violence. Students feel more involved and ready to apply the rules. Although you won't be able to avoid conflicts in school, you can learn to control them. But rules are for everyone. If students are expected to arrive on time, that goes for teachers, too. Respect is a two-way street.

It's much better when you can give your opinion.

That shows how important words are.
Students must have genuine opportunities for
discussion in which they will be heard and
their comments taken into account. Schools
can create those opportunities through student
government, school newspapers, and debates.
Here's an example: Beginning in primary
school, teachers set up a mailbox to help
resolve class conflicts. Any student can leave a
signed note about a problem he or she would
like to see discussed. Every week, the students
gather to read the notes that have been put in
the mailbox and try to find solutions. To deal
with violence in one middle school, students
organized a radio station so everyone could
talk and listen to each other. They were all
very pleased.

*But just talking doesn't work with kids who are
really violent.*

Of course not. That's much harder. Not all
youth have the words to express themselves.
Some use words as if they were punching
someone. They use aggression as a way to
communicate. They want respect but don't
respect others. People in their communities

get tired of their behavior, although sometimes youths are unfairly accused. There's a problem? "It's those kids' fault!" Some youths do behave in unacceptable ways, like accosting people on the street. In some places, violence is very well organized into gangs that sell drugs and commit other crimes.

Many adults are afraid of young people, especially when they are in groups. And they are more likely to behave violently when they're together. Scaring people on the street is also a way of dealing with boredom. This kind of violence can be unpredictable, but it's also very worrisome. If the atmosphere is just slightly tense, all it takes is one wrong word to set things off.

I've heard about kids who killed other students at school.

You're talking about what happened on April 20, 1999, at Columbine High School in Littleton, Colorado. Two students came to school with guns, fired on classmates, and then killed themselves. Fifteen people died. Such violence is incomprehensible and the event sent the entire United States into a state of shock. Too often, people think that violence is most prevalent among the poor and people of color, but those notions are clichés and stereotypes. The Columbine youths were white teenagers from well-off families. They lived in a peaceful town and attended a high school without, from all appearances, any history of problems.

Were these two young men influenced by the violent video games they loved to play? Were their parents at fault for not being more involved in their children's lives? Or should we blame laws that make it too easy to get guns? It's very difficult to explain such behavior.

Maybe these young men felt that society saw them as failures. Maybe they felt rejected, especially by other students at school. Maybe they wanted to take revenge and, for once, to be the strongest—even if just for a moment. Could that be why they seemed to target athletes, who were considered positive symbols at their school? Reports of the shooting said that these young men laughed as they killed their fellow students.

That's unbelievable.

Yes, but it's not unique. There have been other violent episodes both in the United States and Europe. Something quite similar happened on

April 26, 2002, at a high school in Erfurt, Germany. A student who was doing poorly at school shot his teachers and other students and then killed himself. Nineteen people died.

But what do we do to keep this from happening again?

Some people have suggested that schools need armed guards. But that doesn't go to the heart of the problem. Some have suggested a policy called "zero tolerance." This means that if a student says or does anything that seems threatening, the school is required to respond immediately, often by suspending or expelling the student. Other students are supposed to report behaviors that seem threatening. Of course it's important to be watchful. But how are you supposed to know which words or behaviors constitute real threats? And "zero tolerance" also risks creating an intolerable atmosphere, in which everyone is encouraged to report on everyone else. One thing is certain: Schools need more counselors who can listen to and help students resolve their problems without violence.

People who behave that way have a very poor self-image. As I said earlier, they often see themselves as failures and resent the larger society. Their violence expresses a deep sense of powerlessness. They think they're useless and don't see a future for themselves. They feel as if they don't exist in society's eyes so they destroy things to proclaim that they're actually here.

But we can't put them all in prison! We've got to help them find a way out.

Of course. Still, you've got to begin by punishing those who don't respect the law. And the punishment has to fit the crime. Adults must set limits in these situations, too, starting with small offenses. Let's say a youngster shoplifts something from a store. Lots of people see her do it but no one says anything. Doesn't that passivity just encourage her to do something more serious next time?

You've asked me how youth can find a way out. Everyone has a role, not just the young people, but everyone who's part of their lives—parents and other adults, whether at school or in the community. The nonviolent perspective offers three useful strategies.

First, there's the basic principle. All young people need to feel they're becoming someone in ways that don't involve attacking or hurting others. They need a responsibility or a job.

You might be surprised by how many youths can take that on. They've also got to be offered activities that interest them, like sports or music. Then maybe they will be able to discover themselves and develop real interests.

Second, although it can be difficult, it's important to talk with young people, the police, security guards at school or in their buildings, and their neighbors. Because everyone is afraid of everyone else. To find solutions, you've got to start by reducing the level of fear. There are different methods for reaching this goal. Charles Rozjman, a French therapist who works with groups, has developed one method. Everyone gets a chance to talk about their feelings, their fears, and even their hatred. Then he tries to set up meetings between young people and police, security guards, and city officials. They get to know each other but the real point is to find concrete solutions so the community can become a more peaceful place.

And does that work?

It helps people who work with youth to be more effective. They can talk with young people more easily and the police are less aggressive toward them. Agencies that work with youth don't take such an authoritarian stance toward them.

There's a third route: action on the part of young people themselves who reject violence. Not all youth who live in housing projects are violent. And their communities aren't just war zones. Plenty of people live comfortable lives there but some newspapers and TV programs make very simplistic assumptions. To them, violent youth = ghetto youth = inner city = violence. Today many youth reject that caricature. They want people to talk about them in a different way.

But what can they do?

They can work together. I'm thinking, for example, about some young people in a town outside Paris who drafted a "Stop the Violence" proclamation in March 1999 after a man died trying to break up a fight. The young people invited other youths to talk about the statement and come up with concrete proposals. When you get together to talk and act, your words have more weight and you have a better chance of being heard. That's how nonviolent action develops.

Do today's youth know about the important
nonviolent action that young people organized
in France in 1983? They held a huge cross-
country march and covered almost 450 miles.
The idea came from a group of young Arab
immigrants living in a poor neighborhood
outside the city of Lyon. Serious violence had
already occurred in their housing projects.
Cars were burned and young people fought
with the police. On the night of June 20,
1983, the police chased and arrested a young
man who didn't have his auto registration.
When he got out of his car, a police dog
jumped on him. The man's screams alerted
another young man, Toumi Djaïda, who ran
out of his house to help the first man. But a
policeman shot him. Miraculously, Djaïda
survived. The young people in the community
were traumatized. They wanted to do
something to stop the violence. But what?

Several people gathered in Djaïda's hospital
room and came up with the idea of holding a
march for equality and against racism. They
wanted people to stop saying that all Arab
immigrants are violent. A priest, a good friend
of theirs, was there, too. He'd already talked to
them about Martin Luther King, Jr. and had

taken them to see a movie about Gandhi. Do you know who he was?

I've seen his picture. He's a little guy, completely bald, with round glasses. He's not very good-looking. The caption under the picture said that he invented nonviolence.

Before Gandhi, there were plenty of struggles in which people resisted without weapons, but no one called it nonviolence. The word was first used with Gandhi to refer to a way of acting that is anything but passive. Besides, Gandhi didn't like the expression "passive resistance." He developed a theory of nonviolent action during his struggle for India's independence.

For Gandhi, nonviolence represented a philosophy that guides every aspect of a person's life. And not only is nonviolent action a more moral kind of action, it's also more effective than violence. Violence leads you away from the ends you are working for, while nonviolence adjusts to fit them. In fact, the means you choose will determine the ends. Gandhi is often quoted as having said, "The end is in the means just as the tree is in the seed."

What exactly did he do?

In Gandhi's time, during the 1900s, India was an English colony. Several thousand British people ruled three hundred million Indians. Gandhi, as well as many others, had had enough. He wanted to end colonial oppression and set his country free. His goal was to drive the British out, but not to kill them. That's why he tried to come up with other means of resistance.

And so they held a march?

They held several. The most famous was the Salt March, which took place in 1930. The English had imposed a tax on salt, which was part of the country's natural wealth. One day Gandhi had a brilliant idea. He would organize a march to the sea to harvest salt. The marchers covered ten to twenty miles daily. Others joined them. They talked to lots of people along the way and journalists reported what was happening. When the marchers reached the sea, many people gathered around Gandhi. Then he did something the English had declared illegal: He gathered a tiny handful of salt. It was a way of telling the whole world, "We want independence!" People wondered if he'd be arrested. Still, he didn't encourage Indians to take up arms. The English didn't really know what to do, especially because newspapers all over the world were talking about Gandhi. First they put him in prison and then they let him go. They realized that millions of Indians supported him, that what he had to say was important, and that they'd better agree to talk with him about India's independence.

And the march that the Arab youth held—what did that do?

As they got closer to Paris, lots of different kinds of people came to support them. Other youths joined them and their courage impressed many people. Lots of articles appeared about them in the newspapers. They received so much attention that when they reached Paris, tens of thousands of people were waiting. French president François Mitterrand, who had strengthened immigrants' rights in France, met with a delegation of the marchers. Of course, racism didn't disappear after that but the event woke a lot of people up to the situation facing children of immigrants.

That's an amazing nonviolent action. Are there others?

Sure, but telling you about all of them would take a lot of time. Instead, how about if I explain several principles of nonviolent action using examples from history?

O. K. Do you mean that there's a method of nonviolence?

Yes, in a way. Of course, these principles won't work miracles. Their effectiveness depends on your own skill in applying them and on your adversary's reactions.

First principle: know exactly what goals you want to accomplish.

More justice!

Absolutely. All the stories I've told you have to do with struggles for justice, freedom and, in the end, peace. Those are the values of nonviolence. To win, you've got to have concrete, realistic goals. Martin Luther King, Jr.'s struggle is a case in point. To say that you're fighting for civil rights for black people in the United States is a pretty broad goal. But fighting for black people's right to sit in any seat on the bus, go into any restaurant, or attend the same schools as white children—those are specific, clear goals.

If you're going to have any chance of success, you've got to create a group, and maybe several. That's the second principle: to fight with others to be heard and create strength in numbers. The problem is that we're not really used to doing that. In general, people prefer to stay in their shells. You've got to be pushed to work together. But when that does happen, ordinary people can do extraordinary things. Resistance isn't reserved only for famous men and women. It can also involve simple actions accomplished by unknown people. All the nonviolent struggles I've talked about began with small actions. Gradually, people gained confidence and felt strong enough to be increasingly bold.

But you can act together using violent means. There are lots of examples of that!

Exactly, and that's where it gets complicated. There are always people who believe that violence is more effective. In King's time, many black people believed that. You have to show that nonviolent action can also be effective, even more effective than violence.

That's not easy.

No, especially when people have been pushed to the limit and are ready to destroy everything. That's where the third principle comes in: design a nonviolent action that allows the group to show its strength.

Like the bus boycott.

That's one example. But it could be something like a march or any other original action. To demonstrate your strength and your refusal to be a victim any longer, you can stop doing something that is asked of you. Gandhi called it "non-cooperation with injustice." You have to come up with an action that everyone can participate in. Sending black people into restaurants that posted signs reading "No coloreds or dogs allowed" was a good idea. In other settings, people might stop working and go on strike. The French and the Americans have that right but in some countries, strikes are still virtually forbidden. In those countries, going on strike would be an act of resistance.

You know, there is a famous nonviolent strike.

What happened?

It took place in Poland in 1980. At that time, Poles were not free. Communists led the country. The Polish leaders followed orders from other communists in Moscow, in the former Soviet Union. Whenever Poles demanded their freedom, they risked losing their jobs or being imprisoned or shot.

Then in 1980, workers in the Black Sea port of Gdansk went out on strike. They built ships in the huge naval shipyards. They'd held a strike ten years earlier, but some of them had attacked the police station and the police fired on them. It was a slaughter and dozens of people died. This time, workers wanted to avoid violence. They locked themselves up in their work sites. First they decided to ban drinking so things wouldn't get out of control.

In a country where no one dared to strike, this was an unbelievable event. Reporters arrived immediately from France, England, and the United States. The police were everywhere, but some journalists managed to get inside discreetly. It was dangerous for people from communist countries to talk with journalists from capitalist countries. The Gdansk workers recognized they were lucky to have reporters there and treated them like messengers of freedom.

Why?

Because journalists play a very important role in nonviolent struggles. They explain what's going on to the outside world. The Polish media, for example, barely talked about the strike. Without newspaper articles or television broadcasts, the strikers weren't likely to succeed. That's why they greeted the Western media with such hope. The strikers had a good chance of winning sympathy because they wanted to avoid violence. After all, they were facing adversaries who'd already used tanks and machine guns against them.

And did they win?

The strike lasted for two weeks. People thought the army was going to intervene. But the authorities hesitated. Just like during Gandhi's march, people were talking about this strike all over the world, so Polish authorities chose to negotiate. The workers won their most important goal, which was to create an independent union. They called it *Solidarnosc,* or, Solidarity. Later, Lech Walesa, the strike leader, won the Nobel Peace Prize.

That's an awesome story!

Let me get back to my principles. The fourth
one is to use the power of words. We've
already talked about that. It's logical. It's not
enough to act—you've got to explain your
actions. The power of words involves coming
together to speak with the same voice. The
greater the number of people who want the
same thing, the greater the chance they'll be
heard. It's a little like what happens at school
when a teacher makes an unfair decision and a
group of students comes to see her to protest.

Explaining yourself clearly also helps other
people to understand and support you. Humor
is one weapon for arousing sympathy. We saw
how that worked during a well-known
nonviolent struggle in France during the
1970s.

What was that?

It involved farmers in Larzac, an isolated, rural
area in southern France. At the time, people
didn't understand what the farmers were
doing. They thought they were just a bunch
of hippies and assumed Larzac was a desert.
They didn't know that people were raising
sheep in that region and producing milk for a

very famous French bleu cheese called Roquefort. Some of the farmers managed very modern farm operations.

One day, the farmers learned they were going to be evicted from their land so the army could set up a camp. They weren't especially anti-military, but they thought the decision was unfair. They decided to fight using nonviolent methods. But how would they get their story out? This was in 1972. No one outside had any idea what was going on, so they came up with an amusing idea.

What was that?

They secretly brought sheep to Paris to let them graze under the Eiffel Tower. People would walk by and ask, "What's going on? You're farmers from Larzac? Where's that? Your sheep are so sweet. Why are you doing this?" The farmers explained why they were angry. They said they could've gotten attention by being destructive, but they'd chosen to remain nonviolent. Of course, they alerted several journalists.

There could've been people who attacked them. They could've threatened the farmers and told them, "We don't agree with what you're doing."

Yes, and that did happen more than once. Provocation is a difficult challenge in nonviolent struggles. There are always people who say, "Oh, so you say you're nonviolent! We'll see about that!" And they harass demonstrators to make them strike back. This brings up the fifth principle: to remain nonviolent even if you're provoked. That's hard to do. You've got to understand there are risks involved in participating in nonviolent action. When you fight for change, you've got to take risks. That holds true for nonviolent struggles, too.

I'm thinking of an example from the march for equality that I described earlier. Bouzid, one of the marchers, told me this story. The marchers had planned to stop in the town of Loriol. When they arrived, a pickup truck drove up. Three men inside began yelling insults at them. The men got out of the truck carrying clubs and what looked like a gun. For a moment, everyone froze in fear. Bouzid picked up a stone. He said he felt he could've smashed the men. But in a sharp tone of voice, the person next to him said, "Put it down!" Bouzid remembered his commitment to nonviolence and dropped the stone. "I'd just won the greatest victory a person can hope for," he said later. "For the first time, I managed to control myself. I didn't respond to hatred with violence." Suddenly, someone yelled out, "Move on!" And the marchers passed by the three men, who stood threatening and silent.

Dad, there's one question I've been asking myself for a while. What can nonviolence do about a dictator like Hitler?

I've studied that question a lot. How are unarmed men and women sometimes able to resist a dictator? It's true that things often end very badly. Take the example of China in 1989, when students in Beijing demonstrated at Tiananmen Square in support of democracy. The army fired on them. Even so, unarmed resistance can sometimes create difficult problems for dictators. Resistance can be like a grain of sand that jams the machinery they've built to tyrannize people. It's really a mysterious phenomenon. I've tried to solve it as if I were looking for the solution to a mystery novel. I've studied examples of unarmed resistance in Europe under Hitler and the Nazis and then during the period when the Soviets ruled part of Europe, including Poland.

When you live under a dictatorship and terror is everywhere, it's almost impossible to act. Should you demonstrate? You risk immediate arrest, imprisonment, and maybe even death. That's not a good idea. Nonviolent action isn't about being a martyr.

But in a dictatorship, people still take action out of solidarity with others. When you're persecuted, you tend to stick together. People may help you secretly. During Hitler's time, for example, some people hid Jewish children.

I saw a movie about that. I think it took place in a little village.

Yes, that was the French village of Chambon-sur-Lignon and nearby villages. André Trocmé, a pastor who believed in nonviolence, organized to protect Jewish children. The French wartime government in Vichy was deporting them to concentration camps. Trocmé and his friends saved nearly three thousand children who would have been sent to their death. There were similar examples elsewhere in France and Europe. The state of Israel awards a medal to people who saved Jews during the war. The rescuers are known as The Righteous Among The Nations. This phrase from the Talmud, a collection of Jewish teachings, is engraved on the medal: "Whosoever saves a single life saves the entire universe."

In addition to these acts of solidarity, there are also courageous people who try to speak out.

But how?

By using their pen. If they're artists they use their paintbrush. Art refuses to be locked up. Artists and writers are often among the first to express the desire for freedom. They bring down the walls of lies and fear because they want to speak the truth. The Russian writer Alexander Solzhenitsyn was one of those people in the Soviet Union. When journalists find the courage to describe the awful things going on in their country, their words and photographs can have a powerful impact, too. An Algerian journalist, Tahar Djaout, once said, "If you speak, you die. If you are silent, you die. So speak and die."

That's very beautiful.

I can give you more examples illustrating the role of speech and how speaking out represents a victory for freedom. And then one day, words can change to actions. One day, some people are bold enough to go into the streets to demonstrate.

But that's so dangerous!

How can I explain this? They manage to get beyond their fear, in part because they are together. People are not so scared when they're in a group. It's an extraordinary phenomenon. Alone, they wouldn't be capable of taking action. It would be too risky. Imagine facing a tank all by yourself. You'd have to be crazy. But there's something else that moves people to act. Here's an example from Nazi Germany. In February 1943, a group of German women protested on a Berlin street in front of the facility where their Jewish husbands and sons had just been locked up. Of course, they were afraid of being arrested but they knew that if they left, they would never see the men again. They didn't have much to lose, so they yelled until the men were freed.

They won?

After ten days. This is a remarkable story. It shows that even the Nazis sometimes paid attention to public protest.

Something similar took place many years later in Argentina. In 1977 a general named Videla took power. He imposed a harsh dictatorship and invented a new method of dealing with his opponents. Instead of imprisoning them, he made them disappear.

But how?

Policemen and plainclothesmen kidnapped the regime's opponents, whether real or imagined. Their families never saw them again. Everyone was very frightened and as a result, no one dared take political action. The dictator had nothing to worry about—until the unimaginable happened. Some women refused to accept the disappearances and insisted on getting news about their children. People in government offices would say to them, "We don't know. Come back tomorrow." The next day, they would be told the same thing. Soon several of them realized they had the same problem, so instead of fighting separately, they came together. They developed the idea of meeting at a central plaza in Buenos Aires, the *Plaza de Mayo,* to let everyone know of their struggle to learn the whereabouts of their children. It was a crazy thing to do because they could've been arrested themselves.

But their love was stronger than their fear. People called them "the crazy women of the *Plaza de Mayo.*" Every week, the "crazies" came back to the same place. The police intervened, saying, "Ladies, this is an illegal gathering. Move along, or you'll be arrested." "Fine," they answered. "We'll move." So they lined up two by two and walked around and around the plaza. Later, some of them were arrested and tortured. But they kept up their action and today it is one of the most powerful symbols of a nonviolent struggle for human rights.

When people are struggling like that, can we help them? Argentina is awfully far away!

Yes, of course, we can help them—even by staying at home. How? By spreading the word about their actions in our own country and by sending them money or whatever they need. People who resist are often in the minority. To become stronger, they need people and organizations to pass the word about them in other countries. The Argentine women understood that immediately. When they started to fight, they were very much alone and could've disappeared just like their children. They realized they absolutely had to become known abroad. That's why they sent messages to friends in Europe and the United States and held secret meetings with journalists. That's another example of the role of communications and the media. And today we can use the Internet. Little by little, people from other countries came to their aid.

The Dalai Lama, a great admirer of Gandhi and the man who most represents the Tibetans' spiritual resistance to Chinese occupation, is doing something similar right now. When he travels, he tries to make as many friends as possible around the world, hoping their support will convince the Chinese to restore genuine autonomy to Tibet.

Writing letters is another way to help people who are in prison because of their ideas. It's very important to a prisoner—and to his or her jailer—to receive a letter from a person in another country. It means that the prisoner still exists for someone, even far away, who has his name and address. It also means that he faces less risk of being tortured and, especially, of disappearing. Amnesty International, the international human rights group which sponsors letter-writing campaigns on behalf of prisoners of conscience, says, "With this simple pen, we put a powerful and effective weapon in your hands."

You can also help by going to the place where the conflict is occurring. Of course, that's a bigger and, sometimes, risky commitment. To help prevent disappearances, the International Peace Brigades accompany people who might be kidnapped. If a foreign observer is present, it's more difficult to arrest someone. But the observer is not allowed to intervene in the conflict. For example, if someone asked the observer to attend a demonstration, she wouldn't join in but would be very visible and follow alongside with a camera.

Today many nongovernmental or non-profit organizations, also called NGOs, try to sponsor interventions and mediations so people will stop fighting. We call this work civilian intervention. Young people are drawn to these organizations because they want to help and perhaps because they're looking for an adventure. They need to be trained and prepared for their missions under the auspices of a genuine civilian peace service. Working alongside nations, armies, and diplomats, these NGOs can play a positive role. It's a forward-looking approach.

But don't you think that violence is necessary in certain cases?

I've told you that nonviolence can't work miracles. Gandhi was very direct about that. "If the choice is between cowardice and violence," he said, "better to choose violence." Violence is the method of last resort. For example, it can be justified to help defenseless people who are being massacred. The crimes against them may be so horrible and well-organized that we refer to them as "crimes against humanity" or "genocide." We've got to protect those people. But armed force isn't always an obvious solution. How will you intervene? What means will you use? What well-defined goals do you want to achieve? Will you make the victims' situation worse?

Of course, such tragedies don't occur overnight. The warning signs are always present, like thunder before a storm. But we'd rather cover our ears or try to believe we can escape the hurricane. That's what the European countries did during Hitler's time in the 1930s. They didn't support Germans who opposed the Nazis or tried to protest against the growing persecution of the Jews. In 1938, France and England even believed they could make peace with Hitler by signing the Munich Pact, which allowed him to take over part of Czechoslovakia. But the agreement meant nothing to Hitler. One year later, war broke out in Europe.

Something similar happened in the early 1990s, when Serbian president Slobodan Milosevic stripped the Kosovo Albanians of all their rights. With their political leader, Ibrahim Rugova, the Albanians resisted bravely. But if they were to win, they needed help and support from outside to spread the word about what they were doing. That's why Rugova spoke out. "Listen!" he said. "Terrible things are happening in Kosovo. We need help." But no one paid attention except a few intellectuals who passed on his message. Milosevic continued to commit horrible crimes and we missed many opportunities to support the Kosovo Albanians' peaceful struggle. They didn't get help and Milosevic hammered them even harder. Finally, after years of indifference, we had to admit that Milosevic really was a dictator and that only one "solution" remained: to go to war against him.

So do you think the war against terrorism is necessary, too?

After the September 11 attacks on New York and Washington, D.C., it's legitimate for people to want to make sure that those responsible could never do such a thing again. If necessary, that could mean using armed force. But how do we prevent such attacks from recurring? That's the real problem. Unfortunately, terrorist attacks began in Europe at least 20 years ago, long before they started in the U.S. Although the number of victims from September 11 is much higher than the total in Europe, the problem—knowing how to fight terrorism—is quite similar. The European experience has taught us that relying on soldiers and armies isn't the most effective way to deal with enemies who want to remain invisible. The only strategy that can stop them from taking action is to gather more information on these groups and their plans.

Do you mean spying on them?

Yes, in a way. That strategy—which is also called prevention—doesn't require thousands upon thousands of soldiers or increasingly sophisticated weapons.

If an attack occurs, it's also critical to act quickly to protect and reassure people. In Paris, for example, less than 24 hours after the September 11 attacks, all the public trash cans were removed because they are easy places to hide bombs. So we do have measures we can take right away in a crisis.

But I also have to say that there is no perfect response to terrorism. Every country, no matter how powerful or well-protected, is vulnerable. They all have a weak point somewhere. That's why we have to learn to live with the risk of possible attack.

Even so, we can't go around terrifying people by saying things like, "Warning! Another terrorist attack is imminent!" If journalists and political leaders do that, they only scare the public, handing the terrorists a tremendous victory. After all, isn't their primary goal to frighten everyone? Fighting terrorism in daily life means fighting fear. It means just going about your normal life.

But let's end our conversation on a hopeful note. In 1998, countries from all over the world came together through the United Nations to declare the years 2000–2010 as the decade to promote the culture of peace and nonviolence for the world's children. A group of Nobel Peace Prize winners drafted a statement distributed by UNESCO, the U.N. Educational, Scientific and Cultural Organization. They ask everyone to promise to:

Practice active nonviolence, rejecting violence in all its forms—physical, sexual, psychological, economic and social;

Share their time and resources generously to end exclusion, injustice and political and economic oppression;

Defend freedom of expression and cultural diversity, always giving preference to dialogue and listening.

The United Nations has developed a wonderful program, which finally includes the theme of nonviolence. It's a sign of the times. Now it's up to you, to me, and to all of us to do our part.

JACQUES SÉMELIN is a professor of political science in Paris, a former Harvard post-doctoral fellow, and a research director at the National Center for Scientific Research. He lives in Paris.